Successful Selling

IN THE

Beauty Industry

SIMPLE SOLUTIONS FOR GROWING RETAIL SALES, BUILDING CLIENTELE, AND GENERATING HIGHER REVENUE

Jaclyn Luongo

Cover and Interior Design by Bublish, Inc.

Distributed by Bublish, Inc.

Paperback ISBN: 978-1-950282-99-9

Dedication

Sophia Catherine
Thank you for inspiring me daily with your passion for life and smile.
I love you with all my heart.

Praise for Jaclyn Luongo

"Passionate - Energetic - Positive are the three words that best describe Jaclyn. We've been colleagues for 20 years in this exciting ever evolving industry. She brings experience to the classroom, spa or stage to inspire and encourage Estheticians to be their best selves. If sales do not come naturally to you or your staff Jaclyn will teach the skills needed to commit to the sales process through education, support and follow through. Grab a cup of tea, scone and read away!"

– Barbara Devlin, Product Education and Sales, Anna Lotan Pro USA

"Jaclyn Luongo is a woman of integrity, leader and a truly passionate person! Her passion is for the customer! She has represented brands with the same loyalty. I knew she would be a special woman for our Spa and Esthetic industry. Most Passionate Spa and Esthetic leader!"

– Thomas Eramo - Regional Director, Thermafuse

"I was attracted to Jaclyn and her artful approach to skincare at the very beginning of 2000 when she was a young esthetician beginning her career in Boston.

What stood out then and still does, is her ability to understand the needs of her clients and her artful techniques for connecting her knowledge base with their vision for personal health and beauty. She has a unique capacity to authentically guide clients in the direction of solutions and results appropriate for them.

This holistic approach to customer interaction is rare, and is also a modern approach to esthetics, where there are many paths to a single result- we just need an experienced, trusted guide. Whether as an instructor, sales associate, spa manager or the many other professional experiences she brings to the table, Jaclyn has always been a standout inspiration in her field."

– Brenda Brock, Founder of Farmaesthetics,
Fine Herbal Skin Care

"Her talent and commitment to the beauty professional is limitless. She brings integrity, connection and expertise to all aspects of the sales process."

– An G. Hinds, President & Owner of
Catherine Hinds Institute of Esthetics

"Although at first glance 'selling' seems to be difficult to many, it is about simplifying the approach once you know what it takes. That's exactly what Jaclyn has done with this book!"

– KC Harte, Retired Sr. Management in
the Professional Beauty Industry

CONTENTS

Introduction

My career in the ever-evolving beauty trade has taken me to many amazing places and given me experiences I otherwise would never have known, and it all began when I was just a child.

When I was eleven years old, I walked through the doors of Catherine Hinds Institute of Esthetics and enjoyed my first facial. After that visit–accompanied by my aunt Judy–I knew what I wanted to do when I grew up. I had fallen in love with the spa experience–its smells, energy, and environment–and that love fueled a passion that has led to a rewarding life in the beauty industry.

My aunt Judy was the director of the evening clinic most of my young life, so I was constantly exposed to everything beauty- and makeup-related. When I got older, I had the opportunity to work at the clinic and at other spas. I attended community college and then signed up for the Spa Program at Catherine Hinds Institute–the very same place my passion had been conceived! That was one of the best decisions of my life. I have had the opportunity to be taught by experts in the field, mentored by An Hinds. I learned so much along the way, and have loved getting up to go to work every day of my career. The industry has certainly reciprocated the love and dedication I've given it.

I started off practicing at Bella Sante in Lexington, Massachusetts. There, the team taught me sales skills that I use to this day. Throughout the years, I enhanced my skills by working with the Miss Massachusetts Pageant and as a guest artist for Chanel. After opening a skin therapy practice in a wellness center, I shifted my path and explored an opportunity to work with a beauty distributor, which allowed me to travel all over Europe and to forty-two states in nine years as the Senior Director of Esthetics.

My career eventually brought me back to where I started where, for six years, I served as the Director of Career Services at Catherine Hinds Institute. Here, I mentored the next generation of estheticians and volunteered with the Look Good Feel Better Program and Dress for Success with my students.

Although I don't travel as often as I used to–every other week for nine years–I do enjoy touring New England with my daughter. And I still make time for spa day and yoga, maintaining a healthy balance in the midst of my professional life.

With now over twenty years of experience in the beauty industry, it is all I know as a professional. I love what I do and all the people I have the chance to work with and support, and I am so excited to continue to grow within the industry and be part of the evolution!

Regardless of whether you work at a spa or in retail, applying the sales tips in this book will boost your confidence and help you gain more loyal clients, leading you to recognition and greater profitability.

Chapter 1

Why Sell?

Why should you recommend products to your customers? Ethical product sale–consulting with a client to discover his or her needs and recommending product that will help improve concerns–will increase your revenue and client retention rate while showing your clients you care about them all the time, not just when they are in the spa/salon. Technicians who consistently sell home care to their clients have the highest client retention rates. Besides, clients are spending their money somewhere! Why isn't it with you? Two of the most common reasons clients do not buy from you is that they are not aware of the products that you offer or they do not understand the value of professional grade products.

TOP 10 EXCUSES WHY YOU ARE NOT SELLING

1. It is not my job. I heard this often over the years from skin care professionals when I worked for manufacturers. Sometimes, the mindset or attitude stems from how an esthetician is incentivized or perhaps not incentivized.
2. Selling is too hard. This book is a starting point to changing this mindset, because selling can be really simple, very rewarding and fun!
3. I don't know what to say. With the right tools and practice, you can learn quick tips for saying the right thing.
4. I don't have enough time. This is not a valid excuse. In esthetics school, we always teach how to allocate time to do a consultation,

plant the seeds, make recommendations, and close the sale.

5. Why sell products? I'm not making any money. Each spa's pay structure is different. If you do sell, I suggest that you negotiate this, especially since there is a decent profit margin on retail products that the owner will benefit from.
6. They were just looking. My question is, do you know what they are looking for? Did you ask?
7. Our products are too expensive. Never assume this, as each individual spends money differently.
8. I was afraid to ask. We can work on confidence and believing in the products you are recommending. This can be accomplished by reviewing case studies and before and after photos. Knowing your products work really helps the fear of asking subside.
9. I don't want to be pushy. Selling has a bad reputation–that it is being too assertive or forceful. We are here to help others achieve

their goals with their skin. With the right balance of in-spa treatments and homecare use, that goal can be achieved and even exceeded.

10. They don't have any money. This is an assumption that cannot easily be made. Instead of assuming, create and build value. The product's features and benefits will sell the result.

RETAIL SALES KILLERS

Here are some surefire ways you're preventing yourself from building better relationships with your clients. So many other industries would kill to have the undivided attention of a living, breathing, check-writing body in front of them the way we do in a treatment room. Don't ignore this advantage you have in your business!

1. CLOSING THE CLIENT'S WALLET FOR HIM OR HER

We would like to think we don't judge a book by its cover, but we do. Do not shut off the client's potential to spend by prejudging how little or how much the person will spend. Seventy-five percent of all spa/salon sales fail simply because you did not ask for the sale.

2. FEAR OF THE WORD *NO*

   It's one tiny little word with an incredible amount of impact. Each time we hear it, childhood memories creep up to the surface. No one likes to be told no, but clients are rejecting your offer, not *you*. They will still like you and return to the spa/salon. Remember the 5:1 rule: If you see ten clients a day, you will sell something to two of them just by opening your mouth. You are likely to hear five nos before you hear one yes. What is the worst thing that will happen?

3. NOT LISTENING TO THE CUSTOMER

   Opportunity is often missed because we are broadcasting when we should be listening. We should be listening twice as much as we are talking. Your client will tell you what he or she wants. Ask the client what brings him or her into the spa/salon and then *listen* to the answer.

4. LACK OF AUTHORITY

Make sure you look and sound like you should be giving advice on what you're giving advice on. You won't get a second chance to make a first impression. A client's reaction may be based on a several things:

- ◊ Nonverbal clues (hair, makeup, accessories)
- ◊ How you use your voice (volume, tempo)
- ◊ Words and phrases

5. LACK OF COMMUNICATION

Engaging in the wrong talk–kids, movies, politics, or anything but the client's hair, skin, or nails–or no talk conveys to the client that you have no interest in his or her needs or preferences.

6. I'M AN ESTHETICIAN–I DON'T SELL

It is your karmic duty to recommend product. Being a great technical practitioner is not enough with all the competition out there. Customers want the information. When you recommend professional home care products, you are selling the ability for that client to see consistent and proven results to change skin, nails, etc. You are solving a problem and creating a better lifestyle for your client.

7. OVERUSE OF THE WORD *I*

It is the smallest word in the English language. Clients want to know what is in this treatment, service, and product for them. Keep the focus on them, not you. Do not ask, "May I help you?" Clients hear this phrase all the time and will instantly tune you out.

8. **DO NOT ASK YES OR NO QUESTIONS.**
   These types of questions will kill the sale before it even starts. They do not allow for further conversation. We want the flow to lead to another question. The more you discover about your clients, the more you can identify their needs and help them.

Chapter

2

Effective Retail Selling

RETAIL SALES BUILDERS

Here are some easy ways to increase your retail sales today. Employing just one of these techniques this week will give you results.

1. SYSTEM SELLING

   Match two products and sell them together. Think about your client's lifestyle and products frequently used together. Does your client travel a lot, go to the gym, or have teenagers in the house? Encourage him or her to purchase one for home and one for the suitcase/gym bag. Save your client the aggravation of having to hunt for a product by having a spare on hand.

2. SELL WHAT IT DOES, NOT WHAT IT IS
   Talk up how a product will ultimately benefit the client. Use positive reinforcement statements to encourage your client to purchase. Say things like, "I would be happy to."

3. REVIEW AND REPEAT
   Repeat information three to five times. On average, people must hear something at least three times to absorb it. Yes, your clients are there for relaxation but you should absolutely talk to them during their skin analysis, using visuals so they can touch and feel the product. This is especially important at the end, to recap what was discussed and make a plan to prioritize the skin goals.

4. PUT PRODUCT OUT IN THE OPEN

A large percentage of what customers buy is what they see, so sell the senses.

SELL SOLUTIONS

Ask your client, "What concerns do you have with your skin, nails, etc.?" Then offer the solution. Example: "Mrs. Smith, you mentioned during your skin analysis that you are plagued by dry, flaky skin. This moisturizer will deeply hydrate your skin. When you start with our [Hydrating Serum], you will start to see and feel results of more plump, hydrated skin within 10 days."

PART TREATMENT, PART PRODUCT

When your client will experience a noticeable change from before to after treatment, ask the client to feel his or her skin before the treatment and again after. If you have a skin scanner, use it as a selling tool and to educate your clients on sun damage, aging, dehydration and oil production. Explain that their results are part treatment and part product to encourage both home care sale and rebooking.

5. ATTITUDE, ATTITUDE, ATTITUDE
   Expect to make the sale. If you think you can, you can. If you think you can't, you can't. "Success starts with the power of the mind."

INCREASING YOUR BOTTOM LINE: A STEP BY STEP PLAN TO MAKE THE SALE

1. AWARENESS
   Acknowledge the client in the first five seconds even if he or she is not yours. This determines the direction the entire sale will take. First impressions of the spa/salon and you are key. Engage the client and get him or her to connect with you.

2. PEAK THE CLIENT'S CURIOSITY
   Consult with the client and let him or her lead you. Asking the right questions makes for an easy sale. You want to find out what excites the person, not recreate the Spanish Inquisition, so get permission before you start your fact-finding mission. Something like, "Be-

fore we begin, may I ask you a few questions about..." usually gets a positive response.

3. BUILD THE PASSION

Consumers purchase emotionally. Build their excitement through the senses and reinforce with logic. Words alone often fail. Let the client apply samples. Demonstrate the following to make the sale.

- ◊ Sight: video, mirror, pamphlet
- ◊ Sound: moderate your voice, music
- ◊ Taste: coffee, unique tea assortment
- ◊ Smell: aromatherapy, product
- ◊ Touch: safe zone, between the hand and shoulder

Chapter

3

Closing the Sale

When do you close the sale? When the client is ready! Watch for body cues and listen for verbal cues. Your client will let you know when he or she is ready to buy.

TYPES OF CLOSES

1. ASSUMPTIVE CLOSE
   Assumes the client has already bought.

2. RELATED CLOSE
   Once the client has agreed to buy one product, recommend a companion product.

3. **INSTRUCTIONAL CLOSE**
   Tell your client how to use the product.

4. **STANDING ROOM ONLY**
   Limited time offer.

5. **OWE IT TO YOURSELF**
   "You work hard, treat yourself, you are worth it."

6. **SERVICE**
   Give the client your card and recommend that he or she call you with any follow-up questions or concerns.

7. **PRO AND CON**
   This is good when the customer is hesitant about the price.

8. **SUMMARY**
   Group products into collections.

THE PERSONALITY FACTOR

Learning to identify the personality types you are selling to and being "nimble" are the most important parts of strategic sales.

1. TRADITIONALIST

   This client has used the same moisturizer and makeup for twenty years. Educate him or her on how skin changes over time and how different ingredients are needed to maintain optimal skin health. Learn what the client's routine may be missing and add a booster or eye gel to start.

2. PRODUCT JUNKIE

   This client is easy to sell to since he or she wants the latest and greatest and perhaps even two of each. Just be ethical in what you sell.

3. **MINIMALIST**
   This client gets overwhelmed with more than a few simple steps when first committing to a home care routine. Think of a mom with little time in the morning.

CHALLENGE

Think of a few people you know. Identify their personality types. How you would sell to them? Think of how you have been sold to and learn from each experience. Put that into practice, and you will find your way.

Chapter

4

Beauty Industry Articles

Over the years, I have written a few blogs for trade show programs and international trade magazines. I hope they inspire you to love selling and the spa industry as much as I do.

Highly Successful Spa Millennials: The Next Generation of Estheticians

Millennials don't just use social media; they invented it. This is the future of staying innovative, and maintaining retention with our client base.

Millennials refuse to follow the nine to five work dream of their parents, and this thinking fits seamlessly into the spa industry with many locations open seven days a week 9 a.m. to 11 p.m.

They are the *wanted* generation. This is a generation that grew up in a culture where everyone wins a trophy, and this has engrained in them a sense of entitlement. Growing up with a cell phone attached to their hands has also engrained in them a sense of urgency, creating an expectation of immediate responses to their needs and wants.

The beauty industry is evolving every day and staying current with trends is what millennials do naturally. They love social media and follow trends via YouTube, beauty bloggers, and esthetic groups. Consumers, in general, are more aware of current trends and stay connected by reading the same Internet sources, blogs, and trade/consumer magazines as spa professionals.

We, as spa professionals, need to unite, connect, and support each other by sharing our knowledge to create a culture of shared long-term success. Remember, millennials are firmly in the driver's seat when it comes to buying trends and growth drivers in the spa industry; they tweet and tens of thousands listen.

Since the rise of the selfie, skin care and cosmetic companies have worked tirelessly to reinvent technology in their formulas that will enhance a woman's image for selfie "best look" reflection.

Millennials choose cosmetics based on online research, reviews, social media selfies posted by friends, or major stars claiming amazing results. They, in turn, make purchases based on how they will look to all their peeps in the selfie world.

Millennials are also nurturers; they want to make a difference and have an impact on people's lives. They believe they can change the world. Millennials are educated about clean ingredients, and they are environmentally conscious about not leaving a carbon footprint whenever possible. According to a Walden University study, 80 percent of millennials have donated money, goods, or services in their community. Millennials value community, family, and creativity in their work.

Building confidence by combining therapies of health, beauty, and wellness is a trifecta for the future of esthetics. The next generation esthetician is tech savvy and efficient and has a pulse on what is current and innovative.

Hire millennials and learn from them; they can be challenging to manage but listen to them and embrace new ideas. Remember, millennials are your client base, too. Learning what makes them tick will grow your business. It's a win-win strategy!

Spa TALK

I often meet with owners and managers with the same concerns–their staff does not sell. They have so many excuses why they do not sell. Over the past sixteen years in the spa industry, I have helped numerous spas increase their retail business. Is there a magic formula to this? Not really. However, here are a few tips to help you get your staff to "TALK" about the services, and products.

◊ Train your staff, especially estheticians, to learn more and dig deep into product knowledge and ingredients. The more passion an esthetician has for a product, and the more he or she truly believes in the results of the service, the more he or she will "TALK" about it.

◊ Ask for help. Utilize your vendor rep. Your rep can really help keep your staff motivated, educated, and engaged. Use the resources that are offered and owed to you. Ask for gratis, ask for staff packages, and ask the vendor rep to help you run a contest for the staff. The prize could be funded by the vendor rep's car stock budget. They want to see your staff "TALK" about their brand just as much as you do as the owner/manager. They are there to support you and help your business grow.

◊ Let it be fun while holding staff accountable. The more retail that is sold, the more profit you make. So invest in some rewards–gift cards, free services, anything that will help your staff feel motivated to "TALK" about the products/services. Give an incentive for each staff member to upsell services. Perhaps take a survey to research what motivates them. Set team goals per department and an overall business goal to create community and teamwork. Track progress daily and watch the numbers grow while the staff gains momentum and confidence!

Know the top selling tactics:

- Listen to the client's needs.
- Write down what you are recommending.
- System sell.
- Ask for the sale.
- Talk to the client to develop loyalty and trust.
- Don't close the client's wallet or assume he or she cannot afford it.
- Don't fear the word *no*.
- Do your follow up, even if the client did not buy. The sales process is not over. You will have another opportunity to "TALK" to the person again. Send a thank you note and invite the client back.

At the beginning and end of the day, help your staff love what they do and love what they "TALK" about. Be grateful and positive. Bring the entire staff together to celebrate the great stories of the day or week. Give thanks and acknowledgment. Don't forget to "TALK the TALK" and walk the walk. Lastly, do it wearing your best skin, hair, and makeup!

Beauty from Within: Supplements are on the Rise

Nutrition has an impact on the appearance and health of one's skin, and there are many high-quality supplements available today to enhance our health. Supplements come in many forms: traditional capsules, tinctures, gummies, and powders. The "Beauty from Within" approach can be customized to fit the client's individual needs, be it antiaging or problematic skin. For example, these supplements are a great compliment to a series of advanced treatments in active skin care.

In order to be active, dietary compounds must be able to cross the intestinal barrier and reach the blood circulation. This step could be a limiting factor to the efficacy of these compounds to benefit the skin. Therefore, before speculating about the mechanism of the skin-effectiveness of collagen hydrolysate (CH), it is important to demonstrate whether it can be absorbed from the intestine and that the form and quantity can be determined.

Sumida, et al. [32] evaluated the effect of daily ingestion of CH (10 g) on the skin hydration of twenty healthy Japanese women and compared the experimental group to a placebo group (nineteen volunteers). A gradual improvement of water absorption and capacity was observed in volunteers who ingested CH in comparison with the placebo group throughout the sixty-day study.

The following ingredients are also being used in addition to CH as active supplement skin care products in anti-aging products:

- Vitamin D
- L-Carnosine (amino acid)
- CoQ10
- Fish Oil or Omega 3

◊ Alpha Lipoic Acid
◊ Flax Seed
◊ Ginkgo Biloba
◊ Vitamin C
◊ DIM (Diindolylmethane)

Innovative spas are creating customized programs to feed the skin with these supplements, exfoliate the skin with peels or microdermabrasion, and include micro-needling for collagen induction therapy within anti-aging programs.

Estheticians are equipped with products, tools, and knowledge to create customized programs for all clients during each stage of acne (active, acne healing, and scarring) or to tackle a client's anti-aging needs. Estheticians have the ability to help from start to finish, while tapping into a niche market that will create loyal clientele and improve alignment for both services and retail.

Here are three ways to assist your service and retail alignment:

1. Start with surveying clients. Discover what needs your client has or what needs a family member or friend of the client might have. Perhaps he or she may not have problematic skin but may have a family member that has exhausted other options.
2. Ask a few candidates to be part of an exclusive study the spa is launching. In this scenario, the client will achieve results for free or a discount and then could be asked to agree to write a testimonial. Before and after pictures are taken during the study for marketing purposes.
3. Develop a customized program that employs a synergy of supplements, dietary education, home care routine, and in-spa treatments.

32. Sumida E, Hirota A, Kuwaba K et al (2004). "The effect of oral ingestion of collagen peptide on skin hydration and biochemical data of blood." J Nutr Food 7:45–52

Spa

Think Spring!

By Jaclyn Luongo

It's always smart to think ahead–for example, Christmas in July! The same goes for thinking ahead to spring. For some regions, that is when our clients come out from hibernation. They want to be revived with something bright and new! If we think ahead and plan accordingly, we can capture that business! First, let's talk about body contouring. There is a huge trend in body contouring devices, paired with cellulite treatment creams. A series on this–starting early spring–will get your clients beach-bod ready!

THINK COLOR!

A new hair color can brighten up your skin tone. Host a lip and eye event for make-up and pair it with a lunch-

and-learn makeup session. Perhaps include product in the price of the event. Have a local boutique come in for a trunk show or fashion show to highlight the colors of the season. Watch for the spring Pantone Colors, and set the theme of the event to those shades. Maybe top it off with cupcakes to match!

SKIN!

Pair exfoliating treatments with rejuvenating product kits to brighten the skin and get it glowing again. Add in a series of organic spray tans for some extra color! Don t forget to lighten, tighten, and brighten. Spring is the perfect time to offer a peel series before summer begins. Create a beautiful display with SPF. Remind your clients that sunscreen expires and recommend replenishing for daily use and also preparing for the summer beach trips ahead. Perhaps do a sun facts event with information from a melanoma foundation, or get involved with a fundraiser. Brand a beach bag with your business logo.

EVENTS!

For those wellness spas, don't forget about Earth Day! "Think green" and give back to the community! For Mother's Day, it's best to start planning now. Be strategic, and make it special and exclusive! Lastly, do some spring cleaning! Dedicate some time to refresh your merchandise area! Bring in fresh scents, colors, and fabrics. Don't forget about your pots outside. They need a pick me up, too! Small touches like this go a long way. Clean up the wax area and any broken equipment. Maybe even have the staff freshen up with new uniforms or a themed color. Think positive. Think cherry blossoms, bright lips, bronzer, lilacs, and sunshine. It's coming!

Trends in Skin Care Ingredients

By Jaclyn Luongo

As estheticians, we are always seeking the most effective, innovative ingredients available. This industry is constantly evolving. We are in pursuit of the fountain of youth, the miracle to turn back time and slow down the aging process or perhaps the solution to acne.

Each of us has our own beliefs and needs for our practice. Perhaps some want to be green and sustainable and choose the wellness route–organic and natural.

I have witnessed a fast-growing influx of CBD use, providing many benefits from head to toe, topically and internally. Using CBD oil topically on a regular basis for patches of dry skin helps calm and prevent irritated patches from becoming painful rashes. The topicals can also give relief from inflammation and irritation.

If clinical results with active ingredients, paired with devices that are used in the practice, are your focus, there seems to be a trend of ingredients such as polyhydroxy acids and plant-based retinol alternatives.

No matter your approach, each year we gain more and more momentum toward getting results with our clients, and the value of having professional skin care treatments and doing professional home care increases.

Beauty Boot Camp

By Sue Benzuly and Jaclyn Luongo

Event planning for a spa can be a bit nerve wracking! How much will I spend, what will my return on investment be, will people show up?

We have found a great way to partner with other local area businesses that have the same demographics and really drive new customers to your spa. The cost is minimal, but the outcome is phenomenal!

Have you noticed the Fit Body Boot Camps popping up? And perhaps Orange Theory Fitness? They serve the same demographics that we love to have visit our spa. These are women who are not afraid to take care of themselves, and have discretionary income to provide for that care.

We designed a *Beauty Boot Camp*, and have partnered with the Fit Body Boot Camps and invited the participants of their challenge groups to our spa to experience what we have to offer.

Set up is easy, and you already have the tools on hand! We typically set up 3-4 stations depending on the number of massage therapists and estheticians available to participate, we run it from 5-7pm and offer light, healthy snacks. Typically fruit infused water, fresh fruit and veggies and popcorn, (after all these women are spending time at a boot camp, we don't want to derail their efforts, and we keep our costs down by avoiding alcohol and pricey desserts). Another idea is to collaborate with a local Juice or Tea Company to join in as well.

We welcome the clients, offer them a raffle ticket (collect those email addresses) for a door prize (typically an express facial, express massage, or a color sample makeup kit)

Then we guide them to the stations:

1. Chair massage
   - 10 minutes of shoulder, neck massage

2. Hand/lower arm exfoliation and massage 5-10 minutes
   Let the client perform their own scrub, followed by hand/arm massage
   *great time to highlight that scrub that you want to move, or your favorite massage oil

3. DIY Mini facial
   A mini guided facial, client is given 4x4 with cleanser, esthetician selects an appropriate exfoliation, (never a professional grade peel) and then the client follows with a moisturizer. We let the client do their own application, with instruction from the esthetician.
4. Mini Makeover
   We offer a foundation color match and then ask the client they would like to focus on for the night, contouring, lips, eye shadow? If they want to learn more it creates the perfect booking opportunity for a makeover.

Another idea as an alternative is to offer the makeup portion as a "Lunch and Learn."

Have stations set up with mirrors for each client, some products, brushes and disposables. (try to focus on one thing for example; lips, highlight/ contour/ eyes...) Have a lead esthetician or the rep demonstrate a look on a model. The clients have all of the products and tools to re-create the look on themselves in the mirror. Perhaps have a blank prescription pad out for each client with a face chart on it for the client to take notes and write down what they would like to purchase. This is a great platform to educate about proper seasonal skin care as well, and perhaps, have one of the trainers from the fitness center you collaborate with speak about whole body wellness / or invite a nutritionist in to discuss specific topics.

The client always leaves with a prize, usually co-ordinated with our sales reps two to three weeks before the event. This is a great way to get your vendors involved and perhaps even invite the rep to help support you by being there. They also leave with a coupon for a percentage off their next spa treatment.

Selling tips: We create a little display area of the products we used at each station.

Because a lot of the women know each other from the gym there is always a great synergy in the room, and they sell to each other, complimenting each other, talking about what they have used etc. We see sales in excess of $1000 in those two hours, and usually have a minimum of 5 spa bookings before the night is over with about 10 participants

Creating the Ultimate Customer Experience for your Spa

By Jaclyn Luongo

The front desk is one of the highest traffic locations inside a spa. Your clients' first and last impression is with the front desk team. Think about your front desk right now, how would you describe the experience. How would your clients describe their experience? Creating a true customer experience will separate you from the rest. Are you ready to take things to the next level?

Here are a few questions to help evaluate if the team is providing a memorable customer experience:

- ◊ Does your staff call clients by name?
- ◊ When you walk into your spa what do you feel first?

- ◊ Is your team knowledgeable about the services offered?
- ◊ Do you and your staff go the extra mile?
- ◊ What do you offer clients to gain their retention?
- ◊ Do you offer a Loyalty Program?
- ◊ Does your staff know your mission and live by it when in the spa?

I

n addition, does your team practice these skills?

- ◊ Patience
- ◊ Attentiveness
- ◊ Positive Communication
- ◊ Time Management
- ◊ Are they agile? Do they have the ability to adapt?

Here are some tips to help you implement these positive changes:

- ◊ Create a daily check list; a list helps create routine and keeps your staff accountable.
- ◊ Prepare for your clients the day before.

- ◊ Know your frequent visitors and perhaps their favorite aroma and beverage.
- ◊ Use the best resources and tools; your people and your software that run your business are so important.
- ◊ Image is very important in the beauty industry. It is so important that your staff comes to work in proper dress code, hair and make-up every day.
- ◊ The ideal dynamic for an exemplary customer service team is to have a Greeter and a Closer. A Greeter is someone who exudes positivity. Implementing the theory that a "smile is contagious". Utilize that staff member to smile and dial, confirm appointments and do outreach. A Closer, has the ability to end the experience with complete client satisfaction.

Lastly, one of the first lessons my mentor shared with me that I still live by today was; Life is about showing up and doing it with a smile as well as your favorite shade of lipstick.

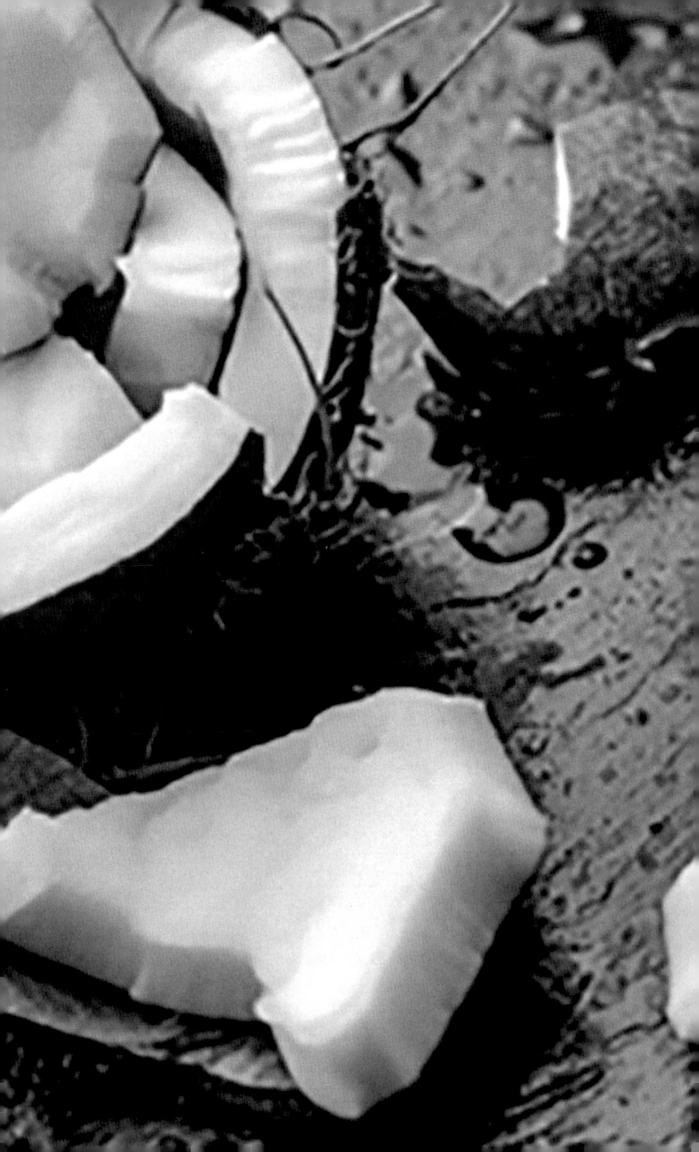

Men's Spa "Likes"

By Jaclyn Luongo

Statistics state that the millennial generation seeks a lifestyle that is filled with wellness, clean eating, and to create a work life balance. The days of spas being stereotyped as a place for just women is in the past. We are all humans with the same stress, need for self-care, and we all have a desire to live a healthier lifestyle and fight the aging process. In addition, statistics show that men from the ages 25 – 44 is the demographic most spas are treating.

Guys are headed to the spa with a partner, by themselves or even with a group of buddies. Spas are adapting their environments and offerings to cater to the male demographic. They are changing the décor with featured dark wood, flat screen televisions in the locker rooms, microbrew offerings and most spas now have a separate service menu exclusively for men.

Here are some examples of treatments that are offered from spas that men frequently visit:

Resort spas offer father and son packages where men can stay, play and go to the spa. Day spas offer a men's theme night, and even offer specific music and refreshments to cater to the demographic. Salons are also hosting father and daughter afternoon events, where the dad learns to braid or do simple hair dos for their daughter. Also, spas put a spin on the description of some treatments to make them sound more masculine, such as "Brotox" or "Manscaping Wax".

Men are doing what women are doing. They are getting luxury haircuts, waxing, pedicures and manicures. Some are forgoing having a traditional bachelor party and celebrating with their best men at the spa. Share the sink with your man, because many have an at home routine that includes exfoliating and moisturizing. Perhaps men are realizing they have a more competitive edge and confidence when they are polished and look their best!

Facials - Men tend to have oily skin, ultrasonic deep cleansing facials seem to be booking more often for men. Men are signing up for skin tightening treatments. Fighting against the process and gravity just like female clients.

Nail services - Spa menus offer pedicures and MANicures which have double exfoliation protocols and also chemical peels on the feet when needed as an add on service.

Wellness - men are visiting alternative options for weight loss and back pain. Cupping is becoming a service men book for back pain and detoxification.

Is the trend here to stay?

Over the years, many men's skin and hair care lines have launched. Grooming products with more masculine aromas such as sandalwood, amber, and citrus have become more popular. There are even unisex make up products on the market for examples, blemish concealers, dry sunscreens and hydration sprays.

20 years ago men made up 10% of the US spa market. According to the *International Spa Association*, 47% of spa patrons are now men. Most likely, this trend will continue. This seems like reason enough for spas to create a welcoming atmosphere where men can still feel like men while in a pampering environment. If spas continue to do this, I forecast the percentage will increase even more. Spa owners nationwide are expanding what services and treatments they offer to be able to capitalize on this trend.

Conclusion

It was a pleasure to share my journey in the beauty industry with you. I feel I have only just begun. I encourage you to think big, have an impact, and leave a legacy! Never stop learning, evolving, and growing!

About the Author

Jaclyn Luongo is a leader of innovation in the beauty industry with over twenty years of experience as a licensed esthetician, makeup artist, esthetic instructor, beauty blogger, business consultant, regional sales manager, and (currently) academy director.

She has trained in Europe and Los Angeles with celebrity makeup artists and skin specialists and has worked with some of New England's top resorts and day spas as well as Miss Teen USA pageant contestants. Luongo has appeared on *The Industry* as a guest beauty expert, has been a guest speaker for the Dress for Success Organization, and was featured in *Pulse* twice within two years.

Luongo has volunteered for the Blue Ocean Society 2017, American Cancer Society's Look Good Feel Better Program since 2002, and ISPA since 2007. She was nominated to join ISPA's board of directors in 2012, 2017, and 2019. She has also served as a program advisory board member at Catherine Hinds Institute of Esthetics for 12 years. She joined the board of directors for the Melanoma Education Foundation in 2016 and NASPRO Association in 2017.

Made in the USA
Columbia, SC
19 July 2021